NARCISSUS AMERICANA

Miller Williams Poetry Series
EDITED BY BILLY COLLINS

Narcissus Americana

POEMS BY
TRAVIS MOSSOTTI

The University of Arkansas Press
Fayetteville
2018

SERIES EDITOR'S PREFACE

When the University of Arkansas Press asked if I would act as editor for the coming year's annual poetry prize named in honor of Miller Williams—the long-time director of the press and its poetry program—I was quick to accept. Since 1988 when he published my first full-length book, *The Apple That Astonished Paris,* I have felt indebted to Miller, who died in January 2015 at the age of eighty-four. From the beginning of his time at the press, it was Miller's practice to publish one poet's first book every year. Then in 1990 this commitment was formalized when Miller awarded the first Arkansas Poetry Prize. Fittingly, it was renamed the Miller Williams Poetry Prize after his retirement.

When Miller first spotted my poetry, I was forty-six years old with two chapbooks only. Not a pretty sight.

I have him to thank for first carrying me across that critical line dividing *no book* from *book*, thus turning me, at last, into a "published poet." I was especially eager to take on the task of selecting books (with the assistance of many invaluable screeners) for the Miller Williams Poetry Prize because it is a publication prize, which may bring to light other first books.

Miller Williams was more than my first editor. Over the years, he and I became friends, but even before my involvement with the press, he served as a kind of literary father to me. His straightforward, sometimes folksy, sometimes witty and always trenchant poems became to me models of how poems could sound and how they could go. He was one of the poets who showed me that humor could be a legitimate mode in poetry—that a poem could be humorous without being silly or merely comical. He also showed me that a plain-spoken poem did not have to be imaginatively plain. Younger poets today could learn much from his example, as I did.

Given his extensive and distinguished career, it's surprising that Miller didn't enjoy a more prominent position on the American literary map. As his daughter became well-known as a singer and recording artist, Miller became known to many as the father of Lucinda Williams. Miller and Lucinda even appeared on stage together several times performing a father-daughter act of song and poetry. And Miller enjoyed a bright, shining moment when Bill Clinton chose him to be the inaugural poet at his second inauguration in 1997. The poem he wrote for that day, "Of History and Hope," is a meditation on how "we have memorized America." In turning to the children of our country he broadens a nursery rhyme question by asking "How does our garden grow?" Occasional poems, especially for occasions of such importance, are notoriously difficult—some would say impossible—to write with success. But Miller rose to this lofty occasion and produced a winner. His confident reading of the poem before the nation added cultural and emotional weight to the morning's ceremony.

Apart from such public recognitions, most would agree that Miller's fuller legacy lies in his teaching and publishing career, which covered four decades. In that time, he published over a dozen books of his own poetry and literary theory. His literary work as poet and editor is what will speak for Miller in the years to come. The qualities of his poems make them immediately likeable and pleasurable. They sound as if they were spoken, not just written, and they show a courteous, engaging awareness of the presence of a reader. Miller knew that the idea behind a good poem is to make the reader feel something, rather than to merely display the poet's emotional state, which usually boils down to some form of misery. Miller also possessed the authority of experience to produce poems that were just plain wise.

With these attributes in mind, I began the judging of this year's prize. On the lookout for poems that Miller would approve of, that is, poems that seemed to be consciously or unconsciously in the Miller Williams School, I read and read. But in reading these scores of manuscripts, I realized that applying such narrow criteria would be selling Miller short. His tastes in poetry were clearly broader than the stylistic territory of his own verse; he published poets as different from one another as John Ciardi and Jimmy Carter. I readjusted and began to look for poems I thought Miller would delight in reading, instead of echoes of his own poems. Broadening the field of judgment brought happy results. It took some second-guessing, but I'm confident that Miller would enthusiastically approve of this year's selections. The work of three very different poets, who have readability, freshness of language, and seriousness of intent in common, stood out from the stack of submissions.

Roy Bentley is a child of the movies. In one of the poems in *Walking with Eve in the Loved City*, this self-described "fat-kid eighth grader" is watching *Bullitt* for the third time straight while an impartial usher looks on. The distance between this Ohio boy stuffing himself with popcorn and Steve McQueen gunning his Mustang GT 390 collapses as the poem rises to an ecstatic celebration of "a communion of terrific car chases wherein thunderous / algorithms of horsepower rule." In another poem, the hormonal uptick of adolescence caused by attending "Sex Ed classes / with our dads" is registered while the speaker watches *Son of Frankenstein* in his "pj's at Gary Laberman's house on Comanche Drive." When he and his friends become sexually active, the poet is certain, "townspeople will start lighting torches." These poems get where they're going by way of long, loopy sentences dotted with references to high and low culture. Helpfully, Bentley is fond of titles that inform and orient the reader rather than obstruct entry to the poem. I appreciated "Saturday Afternoon at the Midland Theatre in Newark, Ohio" almost as much as I did "Ringo Starr Answers Questions on *Larry King Live* about the

Death of George Harrison." And poems about Rimbaud and Robert E. Lee anchor us in history then set us adrift in the poet's revisionist take on these glorified figures. This is a lively collection that instructs, delights, and uplifts.

When asked how to account for the distinctive guitar work of the Rolling Stones, Ron Wood said, "I think it's a bit like the ancient art of weaving." This is a skill that Scott Cunningham knows well (and even acknowledges in an epigraph), for several of his poems make a variety of designs by braiding together strands of their own lines. In one poem titled "Fugue 52" (implying there are more to come), and in another, a sonnet sequence titled "Now a Word about Twentieth-Century Music," repeated lines are used as threads and connective tissue to hold the poems in tight order. That Morton Feldman, the composer, makes Zelig-like appearances in both of these poems should come as no coincidence because the poems themselves exhibit a musical structure, though thankfully not as complexly experimental as that of a Feldman composition. The collection, *Ya Te Veo,* offers many other delights including a wiggy explanation of how the New York School was formed and an updated, parodic version of "Dover Beach" that comes out of the box with "The sea is a bomb tonight." Also notable is a poem about a victim of the Salem witch trials, Giles Corey, who was put to death by a now mercifully shelved method called "pressing," in which the victim lies under a board, which is then loaded with heavier and heavier stones until a confession or death is achieved. "More weight," Corey memorably demands from his executioners. And don't miss "Poems about Concentration for People Who Can't Concentrate," perhaps a distant cousin of Geoff Dyer's essay collection *Yoga for People Who Can't be Bothered to Do It.* A sample: "You're at your desk. / You can't concentrate. / Imagine if not concentrating / was concentrating." In sum, a distinctive collection by a very savvy poet.

What often lures us into poems and keeps our interest is the poet's sensibility, that intangible element that arises from a poet's tone, his or her verbal personality. That is what hooked me when I began to read *Narcissus Americana*. Travis Mossotti's tone is a mixture of irony and true feeling, or rather a balancing act between the cool of one and the warmth of the other. Here's a poet who laments the absence of poets getting drunk in their poems, "like William Matthews did." A smart, informed melancholia can be found in many of these poems, including an exclamatory ode to condoms that is peppered with Shelley-like *O*s, and a poem detailing an encounter at a concert with a woman whose life and body are ruined by meth—a poem that ends surprisingly with the ceiling of the famous chapel whose name rhymes with hers: *Christine*. I trust this poet who can tell the tenor from the vehicle and whose poem "Cigar" shows us that many times a cigar is not just a cigar. Mossotti can also produce a narrative adventure, as he does in "Abandoned Quarry," where diving underwater at night conveys a cinematic level of excitement and tension. Producing poems that are clear and mysterious, funny and serious, Travis Mossotti is one of a thriving group of American poets writing these days whose work exposes the mendacity of those who cite "difficulty" as an excuse for not reading poetry.

In short, we have here a gathering of poets whose work, I think, would have fully engaged and gladdened Miller Williams. Because I have sat with him there, I can picture Miller in his study turning these pages, maybe stopping to make a pencil note in a margin. Miller's hope, of course, was that the poems published in this series would find a broad readership, ready to be delighted and inspired. I join my old friend and editor in that wish.

Billy Collins

ACKNOWLEDGMENTS

A special thanks to the following publications, where some of these poems appeared (some in slightly different versions): *Antioch Review:* "Cigar"; *Atticus Review:* "Putting Money First"; *Barely South Review:* "Kingdom Condom" & "Cruising Altitude"; *Beloit Poetry Journal:* "About the Living"; *Big Muddy Review:* "On Being Here"; *Cincinnati Review:* "One Act: Opening Night"; *Crab Orchard Review:* "Déjà Entendu"; *Cumberland River Review:* "The Nature of Mannequins"; *Denver Quarterly:* "Sacrificial Poem"; *Fugue:* "Modern Agriculture"; *Hotel Amerika:* "The Caretaker's Resignation"; *Michigan Quarterly Review:* "Translator's Note"; *Moon City Review:* "Narcissus Americana"; *Natural Bridge:* "The Abandoned Quarry"; *New Welsh Review (UK):* "Going Home Again"; *Poet Lore:* "Foreclosure"; *Poetry Ireland Review:* "Mourning Heather"; *Rattle:* "Yesterday"; *Salamander:* "From the Treadmill"; *Smartish Pace:* "Fake Flowers"; *Sou'wester:* "The Mulberry Tree"; *Tar River Poetry:* "Black Hole Camaro Enters the Mojave"; *The Southern Review:* "The Colony at Malibu"; *Washington Square Review:* "The Escape Artist."

Particular gratitude goes out to: Kerry James Evans, James Crews, Justin Phillip Reed, Timothy Shea, Erin Quick, Lindsay Mossotti, Mark Brewin, Hannah New, Amie Whittemore, Richard Newman, Timothy Green, Steven Schroeder, Jazzy Danziger, Lizzy Petersen, Jenny Mueller, Stefene Russell, Connie Motoki, Renee Summer Evans, Jack and Mary Webb, and Stephanie Schlaifer; to Lionel Cuillé, Emily Thompson and Le Centre Francophone; to David Clewell, Rodney Jones, Allison Joseph, Edward Brunner and Jon Tribble; to Billy Collins, D.S. Cunningham and all the good folks at the University of Arkansas Press; to the Regional Arts Commission for the financial support; to my brother

Matthew, my sister Courtney, my parents, my brother Josh
for his collaborative workshops and creative symbiosis, and to
Michelle Siegel for her continued support; and finally, to my
wife Regina, daughter Cora and son James for their unwav-
ering love and patience.

For Allison Joseph, David Clewell and Rodney Jones.

CONTENTS

Certo, se vi rimembra di Narcisso,
questo et quel corso ad un termino vanno—
ben che di sì bel fior sia indegna l'erba.

—PETRARCH, *Il Canzoniere*

A· mer′i· ca′na (-kā′nå; -kä′nå; -kăn′å), n.
pl. [America + -ana.]: A collection of literary,
ethnographic, historical or other similar
facts, documents, etc., relating to America.

—*Merriam-Webster's Collegiate*
Dictionary, 5th ed.

READING MACHIAVELLI

Hollywood vouched for upstart Italian American
gangsters decades ago, but now it's trash day
so I'm rushing to meet the beastlike truck
whose arm reaches out to grab and lift and shake.
Plastic bags fall soft as goose down pillows
and sag into the pile with the same aggrieved sigh
my grandfather gave as he sank into the couch
after his last Christmas dinner. My grandfather,
who was not the don or emperor of anything,
listened to Huey Long tell the whole world
that every man was a king and then sat at the head
of his own table like one until he died, as all men do.
Corleone, Borgia, Genovese, Soprano—the names
irrelevant. There is always another rising up and
claiming a throne to hoist himself upon. Always
this same ruthless hunger that devours those
who are foolish enough to try and feed it. Always
the garbage heap of poverty from which he rises
to rule his small piece, to plant his name and slaughter
the senate and threaten to trample the weak. Always
he steps into the role of antihero and becomes
a villain whose ring we can't help but bow to kiss.

THE COLONY AT MALIBU

Glassy eyed on Scotch, my brother and I watched
the electric faces of waves, and I said that nobody
really gets drunk in poems anymore and gets away

with it. Not like William Matthews did. But we
are drunk, he said, and getting away with it
at this borrowed château in the colony.

We all harbor a private sadness, I said.
Melancholia, he said. Melancholia, I said.
Melancholia, confirmed the moon in Morse code,

and the ocean must've known what it felt like—each
wave another failed attempt at becoming. People here,
I said, must take great pride   in the celebrated virgins

of Pepperdine   who graze in the pasture
of finance and architecture   for all of the practical
reasons. Was that Keats? he asked as he poured

a few neat fingers of Glenmorangie Artein.
Keats had the heart of a sparrow, I said, always
fawning over the things he would never have.

Like this beach, he said. Like these waves, I said.

MANIFEST DESTINY

Wherever I am I am
  the revelation,
and I don't give a damn
  about parole violation.

My skin's built with rivets
  and ferritic steel.
My heart's full of spit,
  anger, and zeal.

Much more than a man
  of the lowest class
who enjoys when he can
  this terror, that menace,

just as soon as I enter
  wherever I am I am
the baddest motherfucker
  cause I don't give a damn.

FORECLOSURE

When the bank reclaimed
the house in which I grew up,
my parents weren't ashamed,
didn't board themselves up
inside and wait for the cops.
They were docile as mops
loaded last onto the truck,
their acumen won from a string
of luck—they called it *downsizing*,
used an inheritance to purchase
another family's foreclosed home.
My father dug bulbs from loam
to replant the new place,
and they bloomed in the spring
with beautiful indifference.

COMMUNITY COLLEGE

The '96 Mustang you rock on one spare
tire all semester is what I park next to,
next to you: dilettante who wends permitless
through the faculty lot like a dandelion
through asphalt; student who crowbars
open his life each morning so he can cruise
upon a bulging donut believing it will last.

Without a doubt, there's a shift at some
pizza joint that lures you into the night,
and the sky must always feel like a drag
of clouds that hurts the way overdraft fees
hurt your bottom line. I adjunct my way
three days a week to the spot next to you,
grab my books from the passenger seat

and hike to the classroom we share.
When I get there, you let me sell you
an open ocean. You listen to my lecture
on the craft of sounds and syllables
like we're fools about to build a ship
of words together, like we're tying bowlines,
weighing anchor, and looking alee.

Above deck, you pose in a pastel Polo
and pleated Dockers shorts while below deck
I play resident chef in the galley, sorting
beluga from sterlet on a fine silver platter,
both of us realizing at the exact same moment
that even in metaphors of our own design
we're somehow still the sad fucks who serve.

BRIDGETON LANDFILL FIRE

*To date, all landfill data indicates the smoldering
event is contained in the solid waste cell and has not
impacted the adjacent radioactive cell.*

—US DEPARTMENT OF NATURAL RESOURCES

Maybe we all need a history lesson
so we're not so besmirched by the fiery season,
so we don't grow by accident into doddering old fools.

There's no need to come to Missouri to smell it burning—
all those carcinogens tickling
the fuse in your spine, your spine—

because your land is just as fucked as mine.
At night the lamps are lit from fumes
licking the juice of a cantaloupe rind,

and if the wind shifts just right, it does so because
the earth is still happy to be alive,
because our kids are meant to blaze up radioactive,

because the urge to procreate overwhelms us.
When the ground loses its footing
                              and sinks, it means

the subterranean burning has formed a pocket,
which is like an eye buckling in its socket.
Let's tote some of this fire to Cape Canaveral,

wheel out a giant rocket,
and custom fit it with our land. Let's set
a timer to ignite the heavens. Let's take

our sweet time counting down together.

NATURAL SELECTION

Wisdom teaches that birds in the house mean death.
If you leave the flue open, they'll flutter down
the chimney. Sometimes you can smoke them out
while other times you cannot. Termites are obvious.
The elephant in the living room is less so.
Although we rarely discuss it, there is a sense
that domestication is the fourth miracle we seek
in an order that goes: water, fire, food, shelter.
For cats and dogs it must be strange to imagine things.
Larger versions of themselves would eat the humans
who scoop dry chow into their bowls. They must,
from time to time, sit in the window after tonguing
themselves clean and see the neighborhood strays
wandering the night blackened street. They must have
etiquette.   They must have superstitions
so painfully consistent the only word for it is religion.

BLACK HOLE CAMARO
ENTERS THE MOJAVE

What thrives in this desert does so out of spite
or vanity—cereus blooms coaxing moonblind bats,
Lane Mountain milk vetch pricking along
roadrunner trails. And with regards to survival,
there should be nothing human born for miles,
nothing machine lathed or sealed with Hellfire
piston rings, nothing sand could blister or reap
with a scythe of tireless wind. But this Camaro
is American and therefore stubborn, pigheaded
Prometheus repurposed with a wide-open throttle
and glass-pack mufflers, and we are inside the machine
like a mind in the body of a Mojave green rattlesnake,
inside it taking in the land laid out before us.
This engine that sucks on the cosmos of Barstow
when it revs. This engine, this horsepower
chariot, whorls the named constellations back
to random stipple, starlight, bits of no consequence,
relieved of any purpose or historical context.
Give us Orion, the Seven Sisters, the Great Bear,
and the Big Dipper. Watch dust swirl the air
above our racing stripes. Watch us slither down
into the proving grounds, shake our rattle and unhinge
our jaw. Watch us swallow the whole goddamned universe.

KINGDOM CONDOM

You know, the condom is the glass slipper of our
generation. You slip it on when you meet a stranger.
You dance all night, then you throw it away.

—Chuck Palahniuk, *Fight Club*

Seventh grade health class banana
sheathed in lamb skin, or wallet ridge
rubbed like a rabbit foot keychain.
O luck be a lady tonight! O luck be torn
open with teeth, unfurled like a sail
and lubricated by a favorable wind—
this wind of marriage that sails me back
to the memory of you. . . . O island
of ecstasy! O sun in the sky like the
bright tip of budding chrysanthemums,
those presexual trembles and fumbles!
O reservoir tip! O skin arbiter! O,
O, O, O hallowed and mighty churner
of hormones and forgiver of impulses!
I sanctify you between all moments
before and all moments after: loosed
from the car window for the daytime
joggers to wince at, panties too, math-
ematical remainder of last night's simple
equation, cherub cheeks grown pale
with hangover, beached whale, a heaven
describable, furtive maples apologizing
for rubber trees as winter arouses spring.
The space between the phallus and

what's signified. The insurance against
fleshes. Looped on a branch. Boxed
and wrapped and unwrapped in
the syncopated tenor sax and baseline.
You are not the glass slipper any more
than I'm the motherfucking prince.
You are not the savior of souls
who's been pinpricked by the Jesus
affiliates, even if you are a loophole
in the narrative arc: early melt, river
downstream nobody saw flooding—
reader, have you been to New Orleans?
Have you felt the luxury of ribbed
pleasure? O first world glory hole!
O, O, O, O of the moon shingling
an eclipse and the spasm of light
obscured! Backseat. Frontseat.
Homestead and hostel. Immune
to passion but subject to whim.
Doggie style, missionary, wheel-
barrow, cowgirl, reverse and all other
permutations—trumpet of skin
muted behind this thin scrim
of language, for his and her pleasure:
European pillow top, beast with two,
three, four backs, possibilities as plural
as somewhere in the background a vinyl
keeps spinning out Buddy Rich's big

band jazz: "The beat goes on, the beat
goes on / Drums keep pounding a rhythm
to the brain / La de da de de, la de da de da,"
and all those instruments keep coming
together into a tangled flesh of sound—
another prom, and I'm handing you out
by the fistful from a bowl of rubberized,
multicolored punch—the theme this year
is *Somewhere over the Rainbow* and later
tonight it'll be *I've Got a Rocket in My Pocket*.
O Kingdom Condom, I'm pulling you up
by the roots like I'm a nostalgic ghost
who goes haunting the novelties
of truck stop vending machines: French
Tickler, Glow-in-the-Dark, Magnum XL.
I'm putting my quarters in one at a time
and turning. I'm pulling you out
of your restive and packaged slumber—
the only thing tonight that will come
between me and my remembered lovers.

THE MULBERRY TREE

An enormous bough hung heavy and ripe
over the sidewalk where I passed.
For once I stopped, let go my gripes,
and ate until I stripped the branch,

until it seemed I'd nowhere else to be,
no home, no life, no family,
no name, no soul, no god of which to speak—
my fool mouth purpled, ignorant and sweet.

ABOUT THE LIVING

The Dublin pitch-drop experiment was set up in
1944 at Trinity College Dublin to demonstrate the
high viscosity or low fluidity of pitch—also known
as bitumen or asphalt—a material that appears to
be solid at room temperature, but is in fact flowing,
albeit extremely slowly.

   —RICHARD JOHNSTON, from the journal *Nature*

Not that the man waving me slowly
into the single lane or the men behind
him, for that matter, laying asphalt
in the doldrums of August are aware,
but the world's longest running
science experiment has ended
just as it was predicted to end,
which proved what was already known,
that the road upon which I drive only appears
to be solid, is in fact an artery
or minor capillary of bitumen oozing
me home from work against the flow
of the funeral procession approaching
from the opposite direction.

I've heard hearse drivers in Missouri
earn an average of ten dollars an hour,
which is difficult to live on, even here,
but is still a job with a purpose as clear
as the ozone-stripped sky,
and as the driver passes me with his train

of mourners in tow, we briefly connect,
make eye contact, and he nods
in my direction as if to say
the only thing we can possibly say
to one another in such circumstances:
You exist. I acknowledge this much.
In the rearview, I see the procession
as they are given priority through
the work zone and see the workers
who break and turn to watch it pass.

But there's one man who keeps on after
the others have turned back to work,
thinking perhaps about the living
who follow so closely behind
the dead to whichever cemetery
has agreed to absorb the body
into its rapture of worms.
And even though
he'll probably have forgotten
this moment by the end of the day,
right now he stands there alone
against a river of molten tar
like the gnomon on a sundial
that refuses to cast its shadow.

UNION BREAK

The short ones. Fifteen minutes under a shade tree,
cigarette divvying up the time into flicks, sweat
leaking charged battery acid into the corner of the eye,
the word *poetry* conceding all sense of consequence
to a tool belt, a crescent wrench or a putty knife.
There's nothing   visible about the mind or its
unrealized potential, but there are hammers that will
drive no nails, miter saws ensconced with perfect teeth,
hex head bolts in baby food jars yearning to thread.
Work diminishes the need for work by being done.
Tomorrow is a toolbox that's yet to unlatch itself.
There are billions of shade trees where humans
find peace, but this sure as hell isn't one of them.

GOING HOME AGAIN

Through the empty Scotch glass I see
the bright pink flowers on the fence,
like God's one drunken child densely
pondering the pinked circumstance

of going home tomorrow on
a plane to loved ones left unchanged
in my absence. Let me again
be loosed in that past, the same age

I was so long ago. Endless days
of summer like arrows volleyed
that never fall. The girls I played
my foolish desires with shed

the pantsuits of the present, slip
back into their cotton sundresses.
Across puberty's edge, I trip.
My mother wipes my nose, no less

motherly than in memory,
and I listen to my parents quarrel
over their fading vanity
and money. Sad I'm not able

to understand their words, I cry
and forget the meaning of death.
There's a pink light traipsing by
that glistens brightly on the path,

illuminates the flowers through
the lens of an empty glass. Humor
me, God. Empty me. Let me step clue-
lessly back into past's bright parlor.

THE ABANDONED QUARRY

We'd come only to get drunk and naked,
light a bonfire on the limestone ledge, slip down
to the night-blackened water and pretend

that we knew the first thing about romance,
that our parents' unhappy lives epitomized only
their failure to commit to the principles of tragedy.

Someone stomped embers
while I dove headfirst into the rain-filled depths,
and had there been daylight

I could've shown you the blue Volkswagen
resting where quarry men stopped their dig, but it
was night, so there was only a pale ripple

of stars anchored to a crescent moon.
I knew even then I was a fool for diving so deep,
but I was the son of a salesman,

father who didn't give a shit and sank
deeper each year into his broken life, and those girls
on the shore teasing off their skirts

came from money, so I dove until it hurt,
twenty feet or more, until I touched the car's rusted roof,
until I'd lost all sense of direction,

and time became a thin vein of bubbles
stretching away from me. There was a rumor:
two young lovers swerved off the road above,

landed in this pit, and their bones supposedly
were still seatbelted just below the place
where my hand touched. But this

was just a story, and the car was only a vehicle
in another metaphor—love was the tenor.
I stood on the roof in the darkness for a moment,

pushed away, and as I neared the surface I began
to black out: the entire Milky Way
reducing itself to a single point of light.

MOURNING HEATHER

after James Tate's "Graveside"

You were taken so early
the community forgot
to stop mourning. Most

children quit riding near
your mother's house for fear
of the flowers that rose

in your absence; their colors
seemed quite off, the sunlight
washing them out somehow.

People around town began
handling vegetables softly,
and few of us found any

peace during the vigil held
on the anniversary
of your passing. Make of us

whatever you like, but please
make something quickly.
The air has grown hostile,

and each day (despite great
effort) another trapeze
artist misses his mark.

You were the best this town
had to offer, but now you keep
so quiet. Heather,

just come out and see
how much we need you; you have
no idea how much.

SITTING ALONE IN THE DARK

If there's not enough light to define
much beyond me, you've still got these
autumn maples in the yard that blaze
with bel canto grace and sing proudly
their rustling as a way to keep time with
the flux of wind that plucks the leaves
like a pickpocket might a watch or billfold.
If that's not enough, you've also got
my cigar preening its plumage of ash
and earthborn hints of maduro smoke
that cross my lips as though I were
speaking the language of   Smoke.
All the unlit streetlamps don crowns
while I tend the small fire my wages
have afforded, hoping in the foolish
American way that this match strike,
that this sulfur burn, that this breath
could stoke, that these eyes could witness
an ember that might hurt the dark
just enough   to become a star.

LITTLE SAIGON CAFÉ: COM CHIÊN

It was the only thing on the menu
my tongue could order confidently,
pronouncing it like the French *comme*
chien. It tasted like chicken fried rice
because that's what it was. Shit, I
could've pointed at the damn menu
and saved the effort of waiting for
the echo of the waitress's slight
voice. My previous generation
razed Vietnam's jungles and raped their
daughters and made not one good film
but five at least out of that war and
Bruce Weigl's "Burning Shit at An Khe"
or Yusef Komunyakaa's *Dien Cai Dau*.

You get what I'm after, but there's
always this exigent present hunger.
I mean, I'm busy as fuck these days
with two young kids and student
loan debt and a mortgage and a career
about as satisfying as the com chiên,
which rolled like chicken fresh off
the factory farm to plate to chop-
sticks to all but forgotten. I thought
this poem was going to be a Genesis
poem, like—in the beginning there
was the Gulf of Tonkin and all was

still upon the water, until like napalm
the high tide waves began bull-rushing

the shore. You probably didn't know this,
but I once bowled a 255 game. And that
same year I stuffed a turkey with White
Castle hamburgers. It came out perfect.
I believed in the Loch Ness Monster
for the better part of my childhood,
and that was before the internet. Mine
will be the last generation of poets who
can say "before the internet" and have a clue
what that means. But in case you were
wondering, the key to bowling a six bagger,
or seven or eight strikes in a row is to know
in your heart that no matter how good
you may be in the moment, to be a career

bowler is like being a career poet only
the pay is worse and the fans are fewer.
It's like, once you set your mind to a task
everything becomes relative. Like, once you
lay that first word down on the tablecloth
of the page, the end is all but inevitable.

DÉJÀ ENTENDU

They've invented everything.

—PABLO PICASSO, to his guide after
visiting Lascaux Cave, France

The voice that called you here
is the echo of an echo of an ancient one that
has already started to disappear

from the calcified galleries preserving deer,
bear, lion, and wolf scat.
The voice that called you here

swathed in poetry's inky veneer,
won't curate the artifacts and paintings that
have already started to disappear

from these stony hollows; visitors blear
the images with breath, no matter how delicate,
and the voice that called you here

has done more harm than good I fear.
Please, this isn't an invitation to visit what
has already started to disappear.

Time doesn't need us to interfere
with what water does for free—leave it at that.
The voice that called you here
has already started to disappear.

VOLCANO

The highway near Grants, New Mexico cuts through
a scorched expanse of old basaltic lava
purged from the lips of a now deceased
cinder cone, and when we stopped for gas
at the only station for miles, I asked
the attendant what she knew of the land, its story.

Through the window behind her register I could see
the scrub and cacti taking root, but the girl
simply plucked an earbud and shrugged. Her hair
was black as the earth. Her skin was polished bronze.
She made change of a hundred-dollar bill like someone
still young enough to believe in anything.

WHEN SPRING COMES

There's something heavy in my axe
that yearns to be picked up
and dive headfirst in knotted flesh
twined deep into the yard.

Watch it shiver with each blow,
this green that I have doomed to go
into the chipper, the ripper, the stripper.
My hands don't blister anymore.

WINE FRIDGE

A wine fridge, used gently, free for pickup
on Craigslist; it rests there because, quite simply,
capitalism requires that such novelties accrue
when the middle class suffers a glut of bonus
income come February, and I don't know how
much cheap wine fits inside, but Kendall Jackson
comes to mind as the only bulk white I recall
from the country club where I worked banquets
at sixteen so I could afford to #heymister beer
and gun it across the county line and disappear,
for what it was worth, into a bonfire where
I must've said at least a dozen times, *Fuck
this penguin outfit* or *Fuck those goddamned
rich-ass motherfuckers* or *Pass me a smoke,
I got a light.* Still, that wine fridge will never
cross my lawn, let alone front-door threshold,
the same way my sixteen-year-old self will
never give up chain smoking or believing
in the beautiful death or staring bewilderedly
out from inside my body's bones at what's left
of him that I've kept shelved in a plastic bin
on the unfinished side of the basement. A few
pictures and a journal. Maybe a soccer trophy?
His disappointment will just have to get in line
with the rest of me, because old age crushes
boutonnières into the shape of a wine fridge,
a fucking fridge designed for the purpose

of keeping wine at less than room temperature.
I hate wine. And yet here it is now, smack dab
in the middle of my poem, which is just what
I need. One more absurd, impossible thing
I have somehow been charged with getting rid of.

FAKE FLOWERS

Green plastic stems in clear water
give off the illusion of life
from the dreary kitchen window
sill. Still, the onions simmering

in butter on the range smell more
than real, the still-life of plates
waiting to be filled, the black, smoke-
licked ceiling like a testament

to nourishment. A family
sits down to eat. A painter paints
this scene as though it were real.
Another man looks at the painting

and thinks of a wooden spoon, his
mother's apron slung on a nail
in the pantry the year after
his father stopped coming home. But this

man's story isn't even real.
He slips on his jacket and steps
out into cold rain with a pain
in his imaginary chest.

YESTERDAY

High above the muddiest river you could imagine,
driving towards a home that meant nothing,
or at least next to nothing, without me,
someone was doing a remembrance on the radio

of a Holocaust survivor who, after the war, admitted
to feeling no anger or ill will towards the German soldiers
who'd fled and left him liberated in the death camp:
Guilt will be a lamp by the bedside those men

will be unable to extinguish. Cruise control took over.
I languished between two dying cities,
and the translucent brick wrappings wedged in prairie
on the edge of the highway's lip reminded me of breast milk

crusted to the corner of my son's mouth when he woke
each morning. After the news and an interlude, a woman began
to interview a poet. She asked about his dead father,
a miscarriage, asked him how he translated loss, and I could

hear him scratching his head, nails against scalp, head fixed
to a neck between shoulder blades, and suddenly
the highway beneath me drifted off into abstraction:
hum of a passing car, wind stitching its seam to a river,

sky the color of jet fuel. The poverty of an abandoned car
on the shoulder was no different than the poverty that led me

to donate plasma for an entire year, that led my wife to participate
in a study for a gift card to Walmart: plugged headfirst

into a MRI machine while neurologists in the adjacent
room wearing white coats fed words to her—*picket fence,
lovely, castle, hubris, crocus, grief*—and her brain lit up,
then darkened, lit up, then darkened, over and over,

and they recorded the involuntary responses in the name
of ramen noodles and 30-gallon trash bags. The poet said
he wanted to capture grief in his book, but there were walls
crumbling on the distant horizon he couldn't ignore.

He said *horizon*, even though it was clear he meant only
to touch the edge of what could be witnessed
and say something instead of nothing so that someone
somewhere far beyond that edge could cross a filthy river

on the way to the patch of grass called home
contemplating the words to inject into a machine,
allowing the otherwise inert masses of language to reach
out and touch what was never there to begin with.

SACRIFICIAL POEM

You stand between two better poems
like the shortest brother of three.

Something unfortunate marks your gait,
and an awful birthmark stains your face.

None of these failures are your doing.
Merely an issue of substance matching

form, a cold wind pushing its way through
a forest eaten weak by a plague of termites.

You dream that you were an ode or epic
surviving the millennia unscathed,

but your parents knew better. They
spanked you the day you were born,

watched the blue suck out of your face,
understood the limits of their creation.

RANCHO LA BREA

A lovely bird, with azure wings,
And song that said a thousand things,
And seemed to say them all for me!

— LORD BYRON, "The Prisoner of Chillon"

While visiting the Château de Chillon in 1816,
Lord Byron scratched B-Y-R-O-N
        into a dungeon

I'll never visit. My pilgrimage needs verbs
        stacked like a cord
of seasoned firewood.

        Byron can keep his bluebird
        and Genevois monk.

I'll take this crow and seagull skirmishing
over a ketchup packet
        any day of the week,
        take this blackbird
soaring to the highest tree in La Brea
to savor what's his, what he's earned.

I'll admit it: I flinched
when a tar bubble burst
the surface of the pit

and flinched again
        at the roiling,

the crude pragmatism
of the earth: what
seeped up   versus
what got stowed away.

When the novelty wore off,
I dipped a saber-toothed cat's
maxillary canine into tar
and left my initials on the wall,
just like everyone else.

Outside the fence and across
the street, I noticed a homeless
            man sleeping
next to the Yum-Yum Donuts
dumpster under the afternoon
Hollywood sun who seemed
as composed and austere
as Byron's monk when he lay
        chained to a wall
lost in a dream I imagine
must not have come easy.
Such peace, I thought,

must come from without
rather than from within,
and after a double-decker
tour bus rattled between us—
belly and back loaded with tourists—
I watched a father and son
        cross the parking lot
        to the entrance
        of the donut shop,
oblivious to both dreamer
and dumpster, oblivious
even to me, opportunistic voyeur
with a graveyard of tar at my back.
        Father held son's hand
            while son dragged father
over the asphalt—so eager
to press his face against
the glass and take his time
choosing between all that sugar.

So far as I can tell, nobody
            is actually
from Los Angeles, and the people
        who dream of it and come,
end up dreaming of home;
the Romantics knew this all too well,

at least Keats did, knew that with
the right amount of absinthe,

 Vicodin, and patience,
that with just enough lavender
blooming you could be,
could almost be, anywhere:
Larchmont, Geneva, Provence.

Tell me what this old pit can do
but fill itself with whatever comes:
water, seepage, bees, and bones—
and if a pair of Canada geese
float down thinking they've found
a pond in the spleen of this city,
what would I do but stand here
and watch the plumage blacken
in their landing? Broken honks,
high-pitched and rising upwards—
like seraphim, like castrated pigs—
rising   from a pit
that's been waiting for their arrival.

Give me graffiti or give me ceviche,
just tell me which way

to turn my head
and look: there,

an almost ancient
Shepard Fairey   OBEY
poster has all
but peeled away,

and the building
from which it peels
is becoming building again.

There are artists and then
there are tourists; even the sky
knows how to discriminate.

GREYED RAINBOW

On the long drive to Chicago we got lost first
in Gary, Indiana—boot on the throat, fist
in the mouth kind of town—so we could stand
in front of Pollock's canvas at the Art Institute,
so Kerry James could point at the yellow
troweled over with thick curves of black.

He'd gotten too close and an employee noticed,
sidled us, asked us to step back, told us
the piece was valued at six million dollars.
I said that was the closest we'd ever make it
to that kind of money, and we stayed on
studying the painting while the employee

stayed on looking at us. Kerry James is one
of the few men on this broken planet
that I love; it's simple to say it, even if
the gesture is not. As we stood there scouring
color and brushstroke, I thought about direction,
where exactly we were being led and by whom.

ON BEING HERE

Let's move out to the twin rockers
on the porch. I'll give you the one
facing west, and we can watch together
the yellow lab as he trots down the street;
no longer rambunctiously lean, he wears
the solid form that old, well-fed dogs possess.

We are but minor rockings to him, somewhere
in the periphery, barely extant, and like any
confident neighborhood stray he keeps
his nose up, his pace steady and fixed,
on his way, perhaps, to a memorable hydrant.
You and I know time is valuable, and a poem

can only give so much, but if you've got
a minute, wait here with me that much.
I promise you any moment now a breeze
will cross over the porch to steal a little
of the stuff that makes us us, and in this way
we'll both be giving ourselves up to the wind.

NARCISSUS AMERICANA

At the Olympic ceremonies in Los Angeles
they chose to reenact the national epic, westward
expansion, only due to certain staging restrictions
the covered wagons full of unflappable coeds
rolled from west to east, a trivial, barely noticed flaw.

—CAMPBELL MCGRATH, *American Noise*

Look,
the waitress is new to the menu but she
smooths things over for the watchers on Sunset,
and when our order comes up she's rehearsing
behind her eyes a scene where she plays
all the parts she'll never land—

this land
has pushed us west for too long America,
and this boulevard which wastes into the ocean
waits for the concrete to soften and absorb
the nightmare of our self, which sees itself
in every grain,

and holy comes the Hasidic Jew
into view with his curls and wide-brimmed
black hat   passing below a row
of queen palms, muttering a cantilever
prayer to the air that was once the God
in his lungs

made real with language,
just as the words for asparagus smothered
in peanut sauce and sprinkled with sesame seeds
are made real by the waitress who studies us
as we press green spears between our chopsticks
at Buddha's Belly,

who studies too the flesh
of the palm tree shucker gathering the pruned
fronds into his truck bed—to her, the blue bandana
he daubs the sweat from his neck with must
look as blue as the ocean must have looked
in the prebirth

of this country
we find ourselves presently trapped inside,
like a wooden barrel bobbing its way
along the Niagara River, current pulling us
towards some spectacle too late to stop,
and so we brace ourselves

for what's to come,
imagining what praise will shower down upon us
if we somehow miraculously survive the fall.

JOINT WITH CHRISTINE
AT A TOOL CONCERT

—Tempe, Arizona: October 31, 2015

Oh gods of ink and paper cometh!
Make me put into words this woman
whose mouth has buckled inward

from meth, and let me kiss the purple
flowers tracking her arm as it crooks
open like a creek bend. We met

only a few minutes ago, but I look
upon those marks, practically scars,
and call them the Church of Superfund—

it's where my ilk have come to assemble
and shout infrequent amens. Her
fingers touch mine when the roach

is passed like a newborn at hospital
bedside, and my fingers touch hers
when it comes round one last time.

The band is revving up backstage
when this thirty-two-year-old mother
from New Hampshire tells me she's

staring down a prison stretch after
the show, once her flight touches home.
Listen, whether I recount her affairs or not

reduces that troublesome shit none.
This world of ages present is driven by
twitter shocks and avant-garde mind

fucks, but lo this woman hides her mouth
with lips, mouth with teeth splayed like
shrapnel, and not even I can save the blood

from her veins. It's too late for healing,
too early for baptism, but I look anyway.
Look at her fingers naked and pressed

to mine until all that's left is an image
wrenched from a chapel ceiling whose
name just happens to rhyme with hers.

MODERN AGRICULTURE

A single monarch butterfly, en instinctual route to an oyamel fir
deep inside a Mexican forest, threaded instead itself with the grill
of my Mazda. I found him when I stopped for gas—his one still
perfect wing testing a breeze I could barely feel. Poor thing

must have fluttered out from the fields of engineered corn born
from kernels designed by Monsanto to compliment the flatness,
the harvesters, and the town that looked nearly exhausted
of its rutted charm and families. I thought about the children

lucky enough to escape those fields, dreaming that love is more
than just an abstract concept, learning eventually that every piece
of land goes through its process of amortization. I noticed how
the corn remained in spite of the absence of those children, how

stalks rose in perfect rows and just kept rising like feathers on a wing.

TRANSLATOR'S NOTE

At midnight, the neighbor takes his dog out to piss
(one of those little breeds coyotes snack on),
and I'm outside working on this thing.

Winter is half a cigar nosing ash
between my fingers, and I'm not drunk enough not
to notice a pattern when I see one,

watching those two prattle a small patch of snow
in their own familiar domestic cadence.
He coaxes and congratulates the piss

when it comes and carries the old dog back inside
under his arm like a warm loaf of bread.
I'm descending a staircase of snow.

It's so quiet now I can hear flakes assembling
on the ground as the wind tunes
its strings inside a willow tree.

If the earth grieves, I believe it grieves the living
and orchestrates these scenes
for us to translate into man, dog, wind, snow, tree.

It orchestrates and waits to collect the past tense
in layers (sedimentary, igneous, metamorphic).
It longs to grind us home.

EVEN NOW

When a girl I knew from high school died in a wreck,
I pocket-sipped whiskey at the wake: rasps of nostril breath,
whispered grief, riverlike line that'd formed over the patterned
carpet worn threadbare,   fibers frayed and trampled,
loafer faded. On some level, each death must be   a kind
of victory, but her body lay there like a run-over parking meter,
curls spilling   blondly onto the cream satin pillow,
parents so deep in grief. I just shook their hands, moved on.
Fuck if I knew her favorite song   or where she hid
her secret birthmark, the one shaped like a revolver. I got
like a drunk into my car to follow her body to the grave.
She went into the ground a mystery, stayed that way.

THANKSGIVING

Thanksgiving my uncle is a self-righteous
motherfucker who paraphrases Romans
like he's arrived on the not unholiest of dinners
where I have been drinking not unheavily,
and this sort of scenario seems routine as water
must be in the lungs of drowning men who

take in the ocean and acquiesce. To my uncle
who has turkey, I give you no false praise. I
conscript the miracle of witness without prejudice
and confess your turkey is fucking dry as a bird
this big and dumb and too fat to fly must be.
Tastelessness should mean survival, but it doesn't.

Thanksgiving should mean my cousins catch up,
say grace, and pass gravy,   but look:
they've formed a circle in the living room into
which I assume they're going to pray. Oh fuck me!
and the saints who've been afforded less patience
than I, who've had eyes gouged out with spoons

and been asked to see. I know this is a meal,
annually decreed. I know I should be thankful
for the bounty I've received, but Lord, my kind
is ill equipped to suffer this faithful breed. To
the cousin on his knees, I give you the floor,
as I slip unmissed out the goddamned door.

THE NATURE OF MANNEQUINS

Past the Kangol hat shop, gelateria, and Ethiopian
restaurant, I knelt down to tie my shoe—

water shouldering a coffee cup in the gutter—
and found, as I rose, two mannequins

decorating a storefront window: male
and female, sensibly dressed to match

the red brick and mortar that framed them. If it
had been an avenue in a more celebrated district

with lithe mannequins garbed in luxuries
meant for the aristocracy, I might've contemplated

the nature of mannequins, might've even suggested
that such manifestations were like the sexless

winged perfection of angels, but these two
were not the bastions of some French

designer's spring collection. No, these
were secondhand stand-ins, one outfit shy

of oblivion, a million miles from the craftsman's
workshop; and yet, there they were, immortal forms,   .

fingertips still inexplicably on the verge of touch.

POETS IN HOLLYWOOD

We pedal our bicycles, chrome cruisers,
whitewalled and glitterati spoked,
down towards Pico in search
of carnitas sold in the native tongue

from a truck window. On our way,
we pass an aspiring actress who holds
her pose against the backdrop of brick
while the photographer goes click, click,

click. Together we ascend and descend
the earthquake-   cracked sidewalks
until I'm thinking of unlucky Frank O'Hara,
three thousand miles across the continent

that day on Fire Island when wind teased
the dune-buggied air, and under his feet
all of the earth's violent and angry
upheavals had finally been laid to rest.

PLAYING CORNHOLE

I'm talking about bean bag toss,
dummy boards, dadhole, doghouse,
baggo, or simply backyard bags.
I'm talking about throwing bean
bags at a hole cut out of a piece
of plywood. Slide it up the board
or drop it straight through, but
the game is not meant to make
us better humans. It will not provide
clarity about the origins of human
kindness, nor will it dazzle us
with flights of image or metrical
acumen. It doesn't understand
the inflated ego or the ironic
juxtaposition of the many selves
or the principles which undermine
pathetic fallacy. It's telling us to
run to that cooler over there and fetch
something cold. It's telling us
the object of the game is to score
more points than our opponent
or to lose gracefully. Play to
fifteen or to twenty-one, but
numbers are just how the mind
rationalizes distance between objects
or calculates passage through time,
so it's not worth fussing over.
There is no clock ticking down,

no buzzer to beat, no home or away,
no cheerleaders who live forever
in the rise of another basket toss.
I'm talking about going shoeless
on the grass for a couple hours
of Keynesian leisure. I'm talking
about throwing your bags into a hole
across the yard. This hole might only be
the absence of solid wood, but it's also
why we're standing here together,
bags in hand, waiting for another turn.

CIGAR

There's death and then there's ash. This is the latter.
I follow the smoke of it from a cigar's gray crown to air
on its way to becoming nothing, which seems better
somehow than following the river that haunted Apollinaire:

Sous le Pont Mirabeau coule la Seine,   he said,
and quickly the night came and went leaving his lines
embossed in implacable bronze. I carry the dead
weight of words. Each one is lowered into the mines

of these poems like a miner. Each one has a headlamp
that switches on when I speak its name.
When I say *cigar*, one end grows a little damp
on my lips while the other assumes the color of flame.

THE CARETAKER'S RESIGNATION

I. Letter of Resignation: First Draft

In less than a week, I had the classical frieze
of you that wrapped the rotunda refriezed
in my image, linens coffered with my scent,
pool house up for rent,
and I finally housebroke the Doberman.
Consider it a token of my unspoken
gratitude that I never took certain latitudes
with your wine cellar,
or with your daughter who charmed the villa
one weekend on a whim. She was in on it too,
you know, knows how to keep a secret secret.
I assumed she got that from you.

II. Fire Pit: Owner's Manual

Hog meat fresh from a local farmer's slaughter,
butchered, thick, bone-in pork shoulder
wrapped in paper.

It soaked all night in a cider
pressed from last autumn's gold rush,
Wickson crab and honeycrisp. In the morning,
I purred madrone logs to char and cinder

and placed the shoulder delicately on the grill face.
                              I lowered it
by hand crank closer to the coals,
then draped it with a damp canvas sack soured
by a lemony saltwater mixture.

                    You know the tree that grows
lemons as big as softballs in your garden?

I scooped a few from the ground and scraped
their flesh from rind to bowl then slipped
down to your private beach and ocean
to fill the bowl with seawater and kelp.

Those little touches always go a long way,
and I believe that a meal, prepared thoughtfully,

should take all day,
which I did, intermittently

                              ladling lemon water
on the embers and canvas,
meat smoked with a bittersweetness

more complex than one of your Cuban
Montecristo cigars I tended all afternoon
alongside a glass of fifty-year-old Macallan
poured from its Lalique crystal decanter.

III. Letter of Resignation: Second Draft

If trust is a prerequisite for taking charge
of another man's homely treasures,
                              then I am dirge.
I am the uninspired spear thrust from the phalanx.
I am the reason why you paid a detective to spy
on your wife and why
she happened to be here that week
with the detective in one of the guest bedrooms—
I had the master. That isn't hyperbole
and neither is this letter.
Your summer home was my winter
paradise, and it's time you fully
came to terms with the fact that legacy,
wealth, fear, and respect are only words.
They dissipate once you leave the room.
They conspire to make you weak.

IV. Caretaker's Song

So loose, I pulled the meat apart with two forks.
You probably smelled it from Phoenix
where you wintered at the firm in your corner office,
glumly contemplating another tinted sunset.

I wanted to invite you to dinner.
For both our sakes, for these pleasures

my guests and I enjoyed. We dined
on moonlight. I raised the grill from the pit,
raised the fire from ash with fresh logs and opined
men who cannot enjoy the present:

Such men, I sang, *are deluded by greed.*
They work and they work
until their hearts finally burst,
and only then do they begin to bleed.

V. Letter of Resignation: Final Draft

When I sway in the hammock, I feel trapped
in the back of the throat, like a curse in your throat,
like when stone fruit comes into season
hardened with pits,   which are seeds,
which if planted and tended might grow
to a height, whickered by sunlight,
and ripened apricots might fall on the lawn
to be gathered and blended with jalapeños
and roasted red onions, to glaze
hog meat lowered over coals and draped
with wet canvas and wet smoke.
For us, there never was another season.
Please consider this my official resignation.

PUTTING MONEY FIRST

When you've finally set the pillars
of heaven under the roof of smart

financial planning, nothing can
touch you. Celebrate your status

come Christmas with a token
diamond necklace for the apple

of your eye—let those stones
sparkle and writhe in her cleavage

while the new bicycle honks circles
around the cul-de-sac all afternoon.

Such prudence is the mark of genius.

THE ESCAPE ARTIST

Out of great Nebraska he steps. Out
of some poor farmer's corn
into the netherworld of interstate.

Out of the story he climbs with a fish
in his mouth and into the flesh and fur
and claws of his totem spirit. Out

of the end he brings a new beginning
on a silver serving platter to share
with all the other servants. Out of time,

he borrows his employer's Ferrari F-355 Spider.
Out of the darkness and brooding opera crowd
he hears the name of his wife three years

run off, and a rolling snare drum rattles
the jewelry box in his chest.   Out
of money, out of energy, out of ideas,

he lilts the two-dimensional ship of his body
into a sewer, with no gravitas to speak of,
no ocean left worth mapping.

FROM THE TREADMILL

TV1 has a blonde actress who must be eighteen years old
or is pretending in a music video to play that crestfallen age—
that rhetorical-middle-finger-to-the-rhetorical-Man age—but

the music's muted, and it occurs to me she thinks I can hear.
She waves a pistol at a gas station clerk like she's the bullet
teasing hammer while Jacques Pépin drops scallops into a skillet

on TV2, and an interview on TV3 rolls out a ticker
and subtitles: a new book titled *Gold*, which tells of a vast
syndicate of thieves who've infiltrated a South African mine.

They haunt it like ghosts, the author says, or at least his lips
pretend to say as the girl bursts from a studio lot gas station
into California sun, or wherever, out near San Bernardino

where the land rises from the basin like a sloshed bowl,
spills into Barstow, into the Mojave, dust devils
catching wind like fire in the sun's throat. *Melt down the butter*,

Pépin tells the pan with a wrist flick, *this sauce won't make itself.*
Such a long time spent underground refining ore
with mercury, the men's skin appears toxic, ashen, volcanic,

but then the girl smears her lipstick onto another girl
and the two start playing Bonnie and Clyde shotgun games—
doomed lovers robbing banks with a missing soundtrack.

I don't know how I've descended this far for a reward
so meager—footage of men poised on an elevator platform,
scallops blistered black, bullet wound puddling the bank lobby

floor with one of the girls' blood—but here I am anyway,
burying these ghosts mid stride, shoveling two-point-five miles
of Africa onto their heads and tamping it down. I swirl a glass

of sauvignon blanc against a tungsten lit set while plunging
a trident into these *fruits de mer*. I hold the dying girl's hand,
and she lets me slide a ring onto her finger before I exit

stage left into the cued-up parade of gunfire.

ONE ACT: OPENING NIGHT

The play is simple
and requires only
one actor with no
costume—just a lute,

and a single light
creating a wall
of blackness around
his naked body.

Did I mention he
must be dead? Yes, it
is most important
he not try to speak.

There are no cues, no
script, no audience,
no seats, no roses,
nobody to call an

ambulance and ruin
the scene, no velvet
curtain to open
or close, no encore,

no competition
setting up across
the street, no way to
upstage what we have.

ACRES OF TIME

Whereas the hawthorn marks a mere hour,
        that hill tumbling into the ephemeral creek
takes up at least a month of space. Prison,
        like a black hole or parallel universe, crams
a lifetime into the echo of a single wooden
        gavel. The head of a pin in the seamstress's
hand holds the end of each minute against
        the next, and however many angels dance
they do so for the length of one sad melody.
        The raindrop holds the first sip of morning
coffee. This river hangs from the pendulum
        of a grandfather clock. And that ocean, vast
as it may seem, licks salt from the brief history
        of our flesh that crawled from a blue eternity
onto the shifting and finite grains of sand.

GAME CALLED ON ACCOUNT OF RAIN

The rainbow comes and goes,
and lovely is the rose
impaled by dagger
on the forearm of the beggar

begging   mercy
and money as we leave the stadium.
His eyes are two blue coals
burning holes into his skull,

and his smile is toothless
as a child's. *God bless,*
says the cardboard scrap he holds
even as the wind turns cold

and blows the money from his cup.
He doesn't curse it, doesn't chase it,
        doesn't bother to look up.

CRUISING ALTITUDE

On a flight to L.A., the Grand Canyon visible from both sides
of the plane, my father and I talk Revelation. To him
the atom smasher at CERN is where heaven collides

with science, with particles, with quantum physics,
and he says this much, feels he must remain vigilant
in his watch for the *signs*. By now we're parsecs

apart. I tell him that, because I am a writer
I distrust the written word, that I know the temptation
to lie for the sake of truth, that I do often err,

and that Truth seems as malleable as the Colorado River
lazing its way across the desert below us.
I ask if it's the narrative he's after,

but he says the last thing he wants to see is the story
played out in his lifetime. We are on the wing.
In the event of an unlikely emergency

there are duties we would need to perform to save
the lives of those around us. The canyon yawns.
I ask if his certainty about humanity's course gives

his life some kind of purpose. He doesn't sleep well.
I know this. I quote Yeats. He quotes scripture.
Light balances on the wing and casts its yellow spell

until we're craning our necks to see out the window:
the cryptic path of erosion through salt cedar and pinyon.
This may not be a revelation, but it is a line we both can follow.

NOTES

"Manifest Destiny" borrows its opening line from Mark Strand. "Game Called on Account of Rain" borrows its opening two lines from William Wordsworth.

The interview mentioned in "Yesterday" was an interview on *Fresh Air* between host Terry Gross and poet Kevin Young that originally aired on NPR on March 04, 2014.

"Even Now" borrows slightly from Frank Stanford's "Blue Yodel of the Desperado": "I dreamed / of your birthmark shaped like a pistol."

The last stanza of the fourth section (IV The Caretaker's Song) of "The Caretaker's Resignation" borrows some from the last stanza of "Hymn of Pan" by Percy Bysshe Shelley: "Gods and men, we are all deluded thus! / It breaks in our bosom, and then we bleed."

Dedications (in no particular order): "Mourning Heather" for Heather Norris who was the best my town had to offer; "Greyed Rainbow" to Kerry James Evans; "Yesterday" to Kevin Young; "Black Hole Camaro Enters the Mojave" to Eric Noble; "Joint with Christine at a Tool Concert" to Dan Hager; "About the Living" to Craig Beck; "The Colony at Malibu" to my brother Josh; "Modern Agriculture" to James Crews; and "Even Now" to someone beautiful and young who died. "Reading Machiavelli" is dedicated to DJT.